BELIEVE
in
YOURSELF

A Helen Exley
QUOTATION COLLECTION

Helen Exley

ILLUSTRATED BY JULIETTE CLARKE
EDITED BY HELEN EXLEY

Published in 2018 by Helen Exley®London in Great Britain
Illustrated by Juliette Clarke © Helen Exley Creative Ltd 201
Design and creation by Helen Exley © Helen Exley Creativ
Ltd 2018. All the words by Pam Brown, Dalton Exley,
Charlotte Gray, Hannah Klein, Pamela Dugdale, Pamela
Brown and Stuart & Linda Macfarlane are © Helen Exley
Creative Ltd 2018.

ISBN 978-1-78485-144-6

12 11 10 9 8 7 6 5 4 3 2

OTHER BOOKS IN THE SERIES

Live! Love! Laugh!   The Resilience book   Forever Togeth
Calm and Mindfulness   The book of Positive Thoughts

Helen Exley® London, 16 Chalk Hill,
Watford, Hertfordshire, WD19 4BG, UK.
www.helenexley.com

BELIEVE
in
YOURSELF

A Helen Exley
QUOTATION COLLECTION

*There is no passion
to be found
playing small –
in settling for a life
that's less than
the one you're
capable of living.*

NELSON ROLIHLAHLA MANDELA (1918-2013)

The two important things I did learn were that
you are as powerful and strong as you allow
yourself to be, and that the most difficult part
of any endeavour is taking the first step, making
the first decision.

ROBYN DAVIDSON

All through my life I have been tested. My will has been tested, my courage has been tested, my strength has been tested. Now my patience and endurance are being tested... I have learned to live my life one step, one breath, and one moment at a time, but it was a long road. I set out on a journey of love, seeking truth, peace, and understanding. I am still learning.

MUHAMMAD ALI (1942-2016)

Everything you've ever wanted is on the other side of fear.

GEORGE ADDAIR

Do the thing you fear and the death of fear is certain.

RALPH WALDO EMERSON (1803-1882)

There is a vitality, a life force, an energy, a quickening that is translated through you into action and because there is only one of you in all time, this expression is unique. And if you block it, it will never exist through any other medium and be lost, the world will not have it.

MARTHA GRAHAM (1894-1991)

You must make a decision that you are going to move on. It won't happen automatically. You will have to rise up and say, "I don't care how hard this is, I don't care how disappointed I am, I'm not going to let this get the best of me. I'm moving on with my life."

JOEL OSTEEN, B. 1963

Make a true estimate of your own ability, then raise it ten per cent.

NORMAN VINCENT PEALE (1898-1993)

Aerodynamically,
the bumble bee
shouldn't be able to fly,
but the bumble bee
doesn't know it
so it goes on flying
anyway.

MARY KAY ASH (1915-2001)

Too many people overvalue what they are not
and undervalue what they are.

MALCOLM S. FORBES (1919-1990)

Never say
"I cannot face this."
You can.
And you can endure and succeed.
Believe in yourself.
You are stronger than you realise.

HANNAH KLEIN

Don't wait until everything is just right.
It will never be perfect. There will always
be challenges, obstacles, and less than perfect
conditions. So what? Get started now.
With each step you take, you will grow stronger
and stronger, more and more skilled,
more and more self-confident,
and more and more successful.

MARK VICTOR HANSEN

*Fly free.
Fly high
and far.
Your wings are strong.
There will be times
when much
will be asked of you.
I wish you the courage
and endurance
and the wisdom
you need.*

PAM BROWN (1928-2014)

*One ought never
to turn one's back
on a threatened danger
and try to run away from it.
If you do that,
you will double the danger.
But if you meet it promptly
and without flinching,
you will reduce
the danger by half.*

SIR WINSTON CHURCHILL (1874-1965)

I studied the lives of great men and famous women, and I found that the men and women who got to the top were those who did the jobs they had in hand, with everything they had of energy and enthusiasm and hard work.

HARRY S. TRUMAN (1884-1972)

…so often people allow themselves to be defeated by situations not so much because the situations are impossible as because they believe the situations are impossible.

SIR JACKIE STEWART, B. 1939

You must have a passion for what you're setting out to do. No half-measures. No thinking, "Well, I'll just see how it goes". To achieve anything, you've got to have a major commitment towards it.

SIR STEVE REDGRAVE, B. 1962

We need love and encouragement to grow
to find confidence,
To recognise our capabilities.
And yet, lacking these things,
we can yet discover something worth living for.
Everyone has a gift.
It has only to be recognised.
Believe in yourself
– and see to it that others
realise their worth too.

PAMELA DUGDALE

Believe and you

When you believe in something you create a pathway for receiving it. If you believe life is great, you see great possibilities, you plan for them and, through your actions, you produce them. If you are doubtful and fearful, you shun opportunities, you limp through life, and everything you touch turns to dust.

SUSAN L. TAYLOR, B. 1946

vill succeed.

BILL CULLEN, B. 1942

You have to create your own opportunities... You have to take the plunge to do things, become more daring, not necessarily play safe or copy others. It is being you.

EVELYN GLENNIE, B. 1965

*You don't learn
to walk
by following rules.
You learn
by doing and
falling over.*

SIR RICHARD BRANSON, B. 1950

There are really only two ways to approach life:
as victim or as gallant fighter.
You must decide if you want to act or react.
Deal your own cards or play with a stacked deck.
And if you don't decide which way to play with
life, it always plays with you.

MERLE SHAIN (1935-1989)

People often say "I can't" because they're scared of failure, or are worried about letting other people down. Think about that next time you say to yourself, "I can't." Try to get to the bottom of your self-doubt. Why are you really saying "I can't?" Does it just seem too hard? Or perhaps it might not come to you as quickly as you'd like? Remember, if you want something enough and are prepared to give one hundred per cent to achieve it, then you can. You just have to believe you can, and keep reminding yourself that you can, and be patient.

DAME KELLY HOLMES, B. 1970

You are stronger than you ever thought possible. Within you there is everything you need.

STUART & LINDA MACFARLANE

*People often become
what they believe
themselves to be.
If I believe I cannot
do something,
it makes me incapable
of doing it.
But when I believe I can,
then I acquire the ability
to do it even if
I didn't have it
in the beginning.*

MAHATMA GANDHI (1869-1948)

No need to be ashamed that you're afraid.
Only the stupid claim to know no fear.
Fear is not your enemy but a wise companion,
warning you of danger.
Take the warning and prepare yourself –
work steadily and face whatever comes with
courage.

PAM BROWN (1928-2014)

Courage has nothing to do with your
determination. It has to do with what you
decide in that moment when you are called
upon. No matter how small that moment,
or how personal, it is a moment when your life
takes a turn and the lives of those around you
take a turn because of you.

RITA DOVE

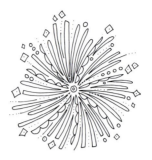

I am the greatest.

MUHAMMAD ALI 1942 – 2016

Consider the bear who never roared, or the eagle who never soared, or the fern who never opened. Tap your Mash-ka-wisen [inner strength], walk through your fear, and embrace your values. Be who you are!

BLACKWOLF (ROBERT JONES), OJIBWE,
AND GINA JONES

Act as if what you do makes a difference. It does.

WILLIAM JAMES (1842-1910)

It's a dead-end street if you sit around waiting for someone else to tell you you're OK.

MICHAEL PITT

If there has been a secret to my success – a key ingredient or a personal philosophy – it is don't take no for an answer when you must hear yes.

JUNE JACKSON CHRISTMAS

Yes, you can say you didn't get the breaks, you had bad luck. Yes, you can complain you were held back. Well guess what? It's time to put all that behind you. It's time to appreciate the many talents and abilities you do have, to start increasing your talents and improving your abilities.

BILL CULLEN, B. 1942

All the strength you need to achieve anything is within you. Don't wait for a light to appear at the end of the tunnel, stride down there... and light the bloody thing yourself.

SARA ANDERSON

Use your imagination not to scare yourself to death but to inspire yourself to life.

ADELE BROOKMAN

*Always
do what you are
afraid to do.*

RALPH WALDO EMERSON (1803-1882)

My own particular bugbear is FEAR. I seem to have been born with this inordinate amount of fear and, in the past, my mind became a master at concocting the most hair-raising scenes from what amounts to a tiny amount of storyline... but how do I deal with the fear? By allowing it, having no resistance, saying "Look, you too are welcome."

When I do this, it comes in like a cat and lies gently at my feet – when I resist, I think, Oh no, here it comes, look out. It forms like a tiger that wants to trap me, play games with me and fully

devour me. So sometimes I choose to let it devour me and it sometimes feels like a fire burning up my body and then it goes. When we can finally allow WHAT is here to be here – know that those emotions will not destroy us – that we don't need to define ourselves by them – thinking, Oh, I shouldn't feel anger, sadness, frustration, whatever it is, we can finally allow ourselves to "be."

CARON KEATING (1962-2004)

Never say that you can't do something, or that something seems impossible, or that something can't be done, no matter how discouraging or harrowing it may be; human beings are limited only by what we allow ourselves to be limited by: our own minds. We are each the masters of our own reality; when we become self-aware to this: absolutely anything in the world is possible.

Master yourself, and become king of the world around you. Let no odds, chastisement, exile, doubt, fear, or ANY mental virii prevent you from accomplishing your dreams.
Never be a victim of life; be it's conqueror.

MIKE NORTON

Hold your head high,
stick your chest out.
You can make it.

JESSE JACKSON, B. 1941

Believe in yourself.
Believe you have something valuable to give. –
Perhaps nothing world-shattering
– Perhaps something inconspicuous,
but important all the same.
Take the skill you have and perfect it.
The world has need of you.

HANNAH KLEIN

The secret of making something work in your life is, first of all, the deep desire to make it work: then the faith and belief that it can work: then to hold that clear definite vision in your consciousness and see it working out step by step, without one thought of doubt or disbelief.

EILEEN CADDY (1917-2006)

Feel the fear, and

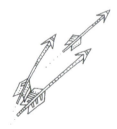

We ought to remember that we are not the only ones to find ourselves at an apparent impasse. Just as a kite rises against the wind, even the worst of troubles can strengthen us. As thousands before us have met the identical fate and mastered it, so can we!

DR R. BRASCH

lo it anyway.

SUSAN JEFFERS (1938-2012)

People become really quite remarkable when they start thinking that they can do things. When they believe in themselves they have the first secret of success.

NORMAN VINCENT PEALE (1898-1993)

You can,
you should,
and if
you're brave
enough
to start,
you will.

A fledgling, teetering on the edge of flight, must summon up its courage and launch into the air.

PAMELA DUGDALE

Low self-confidence isn't a life sentence. Self-confidence can be learned, practiced, and mastered – just like any other skill. Once you master it, everything in your life will change for the better.

BARRIE DAVENPORT

Everyone has inside them a piece of good news! The good news is that you really don't know how great you can be, how much you can love, and what your potential is!

ANNE FRANK (1929-1945)

I'm not preaching for you to go out and conquer Mt. Everest, run the Boston Marathon, or discover the cure for cancer. Heck no. But I want you to believe in yourself, in a certain cause, any cause. Just believe.

To do something, anything; whether it's taking that one class at night school, putting down one soda and walking around the block once a day, or taking some loose change now and then and tossing it into that jar until it's filled and you have enough to go out and buy... you get the idea. Point being: All achievements, whether great or small, take root in the belief in the act itself.

DAVE PELZER, B. 1960

No bird
soars too high,
if he soars
with his
own wings.

WILLIAM BLAKE (1757-1827)

*The best day of your life
is the one on which you decide
your life is your own.
No apologies or excuses.
No one to lean on, rely on,
or blame.
The gift is yours –
it is an amazing journey –
and you alone are responsible
for the quality of it.
This is the day
that your life really begins.*

BOB MOAWAB

The belief that you have the talent, ability, desire, work ethic, and everything else required to achieve your dream sustains you in the face of inevitable setbacks and obstacles.

MICHAEL JOHNSON, B. 1967

If you only ever look to the end result, the ultimate goal may seem completely out of reach and like a huge mountain to climb, instead of a gradual incline that's manageable and progressive. Ticking off smaller achievements is empowering. That sense of satisfaction on passing milestones really propels you forward.

DAME KELLY HOLMES, B. 1970

Hide not your talents.
They for use were made.
What's a sundial in the shade?

BENJAMIN FRANKLIN (1706-1790)

You have powers you never dreamed of.
You can do things you never thought
you could do. There are no limitations
in what you can do except
the limitations in your own mind
as to what you cannot do.
Don't think you cannot. Think you can.

DARWIN P. KINGSLEY

Self-confidence is the first requisite
to great undertakings.

DR. SAMUEL JOHNSON (1709-1784)

Whatever in you
is negative or dark,
fight it, get it out,
put the light on it,
and turn it around
and make it positive.

FRANCES LEAR

Life is either a daring adventure or nothing.
To keep our faces toward change and behave
like free spirits in the presence of fate is strength
undefeatable.

HELEN KELLER (BORN BOTH DEAF AND BLIND) (1880-1968)

The one with courag

If you have made mistakes... there is always another chance for you... you may have a fresh start any moment you choose, for this thing we call "failure" is not the falling down, but the staying down.

MARY PICKFORD (1893-1979)

s *a majority.*

ANDREW JACKSON (1767-1845)

Each one of us has an inner strength, a capacity for survival. Keep faith in yourself during difficult times – your inner strength will see you through.

STUART & LINDA MACFARLANE

It's only the fear that we can't do better that anchors us to a painful place. Fear is our only enemy, our chain to misery and heartache. Fear keeps us focused on what we don't want rather than on what we must do... Being fearful is like living in a prison without locks. We can open the gates and step into the light any time we choose.

SUSAN L. TAYLOR, B. 1946

What would you do i

ou weren't afraid?

SPENCER JOHNSON

Always remember you are braver than you believe, stronger than you seem, and smarter than you think.

CHRISTOPHER ROBIN

We should never give up on our hopes and dreams. The path may be rocky and twisted, but the world is waiting for that special contribution each of us was born to make.

MARILYN JOHNSON KONDWANI

Believe in yourself, never give up, and go about your business with passion drive and enthusiasm.

PETER JONES, B. 1966

The strongest people are not always the people who win, but the people who don't give up when they lose.

ASHLEY HODGESON

Never use the words, "I can't." Say, "I'll try."

RUBY MIDDLETON FORSYTHE

Look. Listen.
Question.
Explore.
You have something
awesome
within you.
Discover and create.

PAMELA DUGDALE

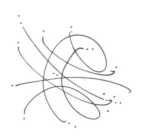

You have it within you to become good at anything you strive for. The thing is, never give up, accept what you are and be proud of it, be grateful for it. But never let it go to your head, always keep your feet on the ground.

BEAR HEART (MUSKOGEE) (1918-2008)

Basically, you have two options in this world – live, or die. And if you're going to live life crippled by fears of your own failings, then tell me what exactly is the point?

DEBBIE HARRY, B. 1945

*Never look down
to test the ground
before taking
your next step:
only they
who keep their eyes
fixed on the far horizon
will find
the right road.*

DAG HAMMARSKJÖLD (1905-1961)

If you have a dream, don't just sit there. Gather courage to believe that you can succeed and leave no stone unturned to make it a reality.

ROOPLEEN

It isn't very courageous to go forth when you don't know the dangers. But it's very courageous to go forth when you do.

KATHERINE MARTIN

Believe in yourself and all that you are. Know that there is something inside you that is greater than any obstacle.

CHRISTIAN D. LARSON (1874-1954)

Doubt is a killer.
You just have to know
who you are and what
you stand for.

JENNIFER LOPEZ, B. 1970

Never underestimate
the power you have
to take your life in a new direction.

GERMANY KENT, B. 1975

The message is that if you believe in what you create, it's enjoyable and people will follow. The talented mangaka should know that otherwise, no one would read or enjoy it. So believe in yourself. Believing in yourself is important.

TITE KUBO, B. 1977

I laugh at myself.
I don't take myself completely seriously.
I think that's another quality that people have to hold on to... you have to laugh, especially at yourself.

MADONNA, B. 1958

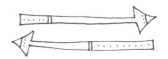

Work hard for what you want because it won't come to you without a fight. You have to be strong and courageous and know that you can do anything you put your mind to. If somebody puts you down or criticizes you, just keep on believing in yourself and turn it into something positive.

LEAH LABELLE

If you are hopeful and determined,
you will always
find some measure of success.
Winning the gold medal does not matter.
You will have tried your best.

THE DALAI LAMA, B. 1935

*Hone your skill
till it's razor sharp.
Practice.
Improve.
Perfect.
Take courage.*

PAM BROWN (1928-2014)

Your plan for work and happiness
should be big, imaginative and daring.
Strike out boldly for the things
you honestly want more than
anything else in the world.
The mistake is to put your sights too low,
not to raise them too high.

HENRY J. KAISER

Believe you can and you can.
Believe you will
and you will.
See yourself achieving,
and you will achieve.

GARDNER HUNTING

You have your brush,
you have your colours,
you paint paradise,
then in you go.

NIKOS KAZANTZAKIS (1883-1957)

Don't let the noise of others' opinions drown
out your own inner voice. And most important,
have the courage to follow your heart
and intuition. They somehow already know
what you truly want to become.

STEVE JOBS (1955-2011)

Honest gain breeds most joy, I shall add most security, when it is gotten with most pain. We look with most delight upon those things which we think to be our own, and we think them most which we have most laboured for.

HENRY VAUGHAN (1622-1695)

The winners in life think constantly in terms of I can, I will, and I am. Losers, on the other hand, concentrate their waking thoughts on what they should have or would have done, or what they can't do.

DENIS WAITLEY, B. 1933

*For people sometimes
believed that it was safer
to live with complaints,
was necessary to
cooperate with grief,
was all right to become
an accomplice in
self-ambush....
Take heart to flat out
decide to be well and stride
into the future sane
and whole.*

TONI CADE BAMBARA (1939-1995)

A great deal of talent is lost to the world for want of a little courage. Every day sends to their graves obscure people whose timidity prevented them from making a first effort.

SYDNEY SMITH (1771-1845)

I want to get you excited about who you are, what you are, what you have, and what can still be for you. I want to inspire you to see that you can go far beyond where you are right now.

VIRGINIA SATIR (1916-1988)

Strength doesn't come from what you can do. It comes from overcoming the things you once thought you couldn't.

RIKKI ROGERS

If you have no
confidence in self,
you are twice defeated
in the race of life.
With confidence,
you have won
even before you
have started.

MARCUS TULLIUS CICERO (106 B.C. - 43 B.C.)

*No matter
how you feel,
get up,
dress up
and show up.*

REGINA BRETT, B. 1956

Each handicap
is like a hurdle in a steeplechase,
and when you ride up to it,
if you throw your heart over,
the horse will go along too.

LAURENCE BIXBY

Courage is taking a step forward
into an area of difficulty
without a solution in mind,
trusting that whatever help you need
will become available.

DADI JANKI, B. 1916

Your self-worth is defined by you.
You don't have to depend on someone
telling you who you are.

BEYONCÉ, B. 1981

Go confidently in the direction of your dreams! Live the life you've imagined.

HENRY DAVID THOREAU (1817-1862)

Believe you can an

ou're halfway there.

THEODORE ROOSEVELT (1858-1919)

The world has no room for cowards. We must all be ready somehow to toil, to suffer, to die. And yours is not the less noble because no drum beats before you when you go out into your daily battlefields, and no crowds shout about your coming when you return from your daily victory or defeat.

ROBERT LOUIS STEVENSON (1850-1894)

*Inaction breeds doubt
and fear. Action breeds
confidence and courage.
If you want to conquer fear,
do not sit home
and think about it.
Go out and get busy.*

DALE CARNEGIE (1888-1955)

If you doubt yourself,
then indeed
you stand on shaky ground.

HENRIK IBSEN (1828-1906)

You may be the only person left who believes in you, but it's enough.
It takes just one star to pierce a universe of darkness. Never give up.

RICHELLE E. GOODRICH

No matter what a woman looks like, if she's confident, she's sexy.

PARIS HILTON, B. 1981

Always listen to yourself... It is better to be wrong than simply to follow convention. If you are wrong, no matter, you have learned something and you will grow stronger. If you are right you have taken another step towards a fulfilling life.

BRYCE COURTENAY (1933-2012)

*If you believe
you're right,
stand up and fight
for your place
in the sun.*

ERIN BROCKOVICH, B. 1960

...as one goes through life
one learns that if you don't
paddle your own canoe,
you don't move.

KATHARINE HEPBURN (1907-2003)

No matter how hard you work
for success, if your thought is saturated
with the fear of failure, it will kill
your efforts, neutralize your endeavours
and make success impossible.

CHARLES BAUDOUIN (1893-1963)

Belief in oneself is one of the most important
bricks in building any successful venture.

LYDIA M. CHILD (1802-1880)

*My life
has been filled
with terrible
misfortune;
most of which
never happened.*

MICHEL EYQUEM DE MONTAIGNE (1533-1592)

It's the people who can turn
a negative into a positive
and bounce back
who really get ahead in life.

MARY LOU RETTON, B. 1968

Each new day is an opportunity to start all over again... to clarify our vision.

JO PETTY

If you won't be better tomorrow than you were today, then what do you need tomorrow for?

RABBI NACHMAN OF BRATSLAV

Character consists of what you do on the third and fourth tries.

JAMES A. MICHENER (1907-1997)

No one except you alone can change your life.

M.K. SONI

*Don't look at
your feet
to see if you
are doing it right.
Just dance.*

ANNE LAMOTT, B. 1954

The best way
to gain self-confidence
is to do what
you are afraid to do.

AUTHOR UNKNOWN

I say if it's going to be done, let's do it. Let's not put it in the hands of fate. Let's not put it in the hands of someone who doesn't know me. I know me best. Then take a breath and go ahead.

ANITA BAKER, B. 1957

In all time there has never
been anyone like you.
You are utterly unique.
You have something to give
that no one else can give.
It may seem insignificant
but it may change a heart,
a mind, a life.
Recognise your worth.

PAM BROWN (1928-2014)

*We are still
masters of our fate.
We are still
captains of our souls.*

SIR WINSTON CHURCHILL (1874-1965)

Give your life to a project
– your intelligence, your conviction,
your ability, your strength –
and you can endure any opposition.

CHARLOTTE GRAY

Keep on going, and the chances are that you will stumble on something, perhaps when you are least expecting it. I have never heard of anyone stumbling on something sitting down.

CHARLES F. KETTERING (1876-1958)

Life only demands from you the strength you possess. Only one feat is possible – not to have to run away.

DAG HAMMARSKJÖLD (1905-1961)

I had to grow to love my body.
I did not have a good self-image at first.
Finally it occurred to me,
I'm either going to love me or hate me.
And I chose to love myself.
Then everything kind of sprung from there.
Things that I thought weren't attractive
became sexy.
Confidence makes you sexy.

QUEEN LATIFAH, B. 1970

If we remain pessimistic,
thinking that we cannot succeed,
then we aren't able to evolve.
The thought that we cannot compete
with others is the first step toward failure.

THE DALAI LAMA, B. 1935

Doubting yourself is like pointing a gun at your motivation.

JOEY GLOOR

Stop trying to "Fix" yourself;
you're not broken!
You are perfectly imperfect
and powerful beyond measure.

STEVE MARABOLI, B. 1975

Keep shining.
The world needs your light.

AUTHOR UNKNOWN

*The only way
to remove obstacles
is to face them
head-on,
just like the buffalo
stands facing the wind.*

GOLDIE HAWN, B. 1945

Courage is being scared to death – but saddling up anyway.

JOHN WAYNE (1907-1979)

If I were asked to give what I consider the single most useful bit of advice for all humanity it would be this: Expect trouble as an inevitable part of life and when it comes, hold your head high, look it squarely in the eye and say, "I will be bigger than you. You cannot defeat me."

ANN LANDERS

It's hard to fight an enemy who has outposts in your head.

SALLY KEMPTON, B. 1943

Always bear in mind that your own resolution to succeed is more important than any other one thing.

ABRAHAM LINCOLN (1809-1865)

I quit being afraid when my first venture failed and the sky didn't fall down.

ALLEN H NEUHARTH

My will shall shape my future.
Whether I fail or succeed
shall be no one's doing but my own.
I am the force;
I can clear any obstacle before me
or I can be lost in the maze.
My choice; my responsibility;
win or lose,
only I hold the key to my destiny.

ELAINE MAXWELL

When I was young,
I thought confidence could
be earned with perfection.
Now I know that you don't earn it;
you claim it.
And you do that by loving
the wacky, endlessly
optimistic,
enthusiastically uninhibited free spirit
that is the essence of style,
the quintessence of heart,
and uniquely you.

CECELIE BARRY

Without a soaring belief in ourself we are nothing. And this belief lifts one person above another person.

IRÉNÉE GUILANE DIOH, B. 1948

And my dad drilled it in my head, you know, "If you want it bad enough, and you're willing to make the sacrifices, you can do it. But first you have to believe in yourself.

JENNIE FINCH, B. 1980

Seeds of greatness within! If you think you have it, grab it and run with it!

DALTON EXLEY

You can have it all, but there are two keys to this kingdom. The first is that you have to believe in yourself. And the second is love. You're going to have to love your work passionately – love it enough to feel it's worth the nightmare of days that are twenty-nine hours long.

BEVERLY SILLS (1929-2007)

Positive thinking is the key to success in business, education, pro-football, anything that you can mention. I go out there thinking that I am going to complete every pass.

RON JAWORSKI

Have respect for yourself, and patience and compassion. With these, you can handle anything.

JACK KORNFIELD, B. 1945

Many of you
Have seen tears
And disappointments.
You regret that which was.
You gaze upon your mistakes
And carry your guilt.
But
Were they mistakes?
Or
Did you make them
That you may learn?

CLEARWATER

In order to succeed,
we must first believe that we can.

NIKOS KAZANTZAKIS (1883-1957)

One failure doesn't make disaster.
Remember the song:
"Pick yourself up. Dust yourself down.
Start all over again."

PAM BROWN (1928-2014)

Don't rely on someone else for your happiness
and self-worth. Only you can be responsible for
that. If you can't love and respect yourself –
no one else will be able to make that happen.
Accept who you are – completely; the good and
the bad – and make changes as YOU see fit –
not because you think someone else wants you
to be different.

STACY CHARTER

The greater danger
for most of us
lies not in setting our
aim too high and
falling short;
but in setting our aim
too low and
achieving our mark.

MICHELANGELO (1475-1564)

If I could give one tip for people – it's not an exercise or nutrition regimen. It's to walk your talk and believe in yourself, because at the end of the day, the dumbbell and diet don't get you in shape. It's your accountability to your word.

BRETT HOEBEL

Yesterday is not ours to recover, but tomorrow is ours to win or lose.

LYNDON B. JOHNSON (1908-1973)

Don't look back. Don't look down. Always look over the horizon.

WILLARD KEITH

Live daringly,
boldly,
fearlessly.
Taste the relish
to be found in
competition –
in having put forth
the best
within you.

HENRY J. KAISER

Optimism is the faith
that leads to achievement.
Nothing can be done
without hope and confidence.

HELEN KELLER
(BORN BOTH DEAF AND BLIND) (1880-1968)

When there is no enemy within,
the enemies outside cannot hurt you.

AFRICAN PROVERB

*The choice to have
a great attitude
is something that nobody
or no circumstance
can take from you.*

ZIG ZIGLAR

The more we let each voice
sing out with its own true tone,
the richer will be the diversity
of the chant in unison.

ANGELUS SILESIUS (1624-1677)

If you can imagine it, you can achieve it.
If you can dream it, you can become it.

WILLIAM ARTHUR WARD (1921-1994)

*However bad
life may seem,
there is always
something
you can do,
and succeed at.*

STEPHEN HAWKING, B. 1942

We avoid the things that we're afraid of because we think there will be dire consequences if we confront them. But the truly dire consequences in our lives comes from avoiding things that we need to learn about or discover.

SHAKTI GAWAIN, B. 1948

We are taught you must blame your father, your sisters, your brothers, the school, the teachers – you can blame anyone, but never blame yourself. It's never your fault. But it's ALWAYS your fault, because if you wanted to change, you're the one who has got to change. It's as simple as that, isn't it?

KATHARINE HEPBURN (1907-2003)

Only you can contr

To say yes, you have to sweat and roll up your sleeves and plunge both hands into life up to the elbows.

JEAN ANOUILH (1910-1987)

When you really believe in what you're doing, you must persevere despite all obstacles.

LEE IACOCCA, B. 1924

our future. DR. SEUSS (1904-1991)

…if you want something badly enough and strive for it, you can do it. It may not come overnight, but your persistence will win out.

BEAR HEART (MUSKOGEE) (1918-2008)

I wish I could just go tell
all the young women
I work with,
all these fabulous women,
"Believe in yourself
and negotiate for yourself.
Own your own success."

SHERYL SANDBERG, B. 1969

Trust that still,
small voice that says,
"This might work
and I'll try it."

DIANE MARIECHILD

Nothing is quite as thrilling as the voyage from darkness to light, from "I can't" to "I can".

LETTY COTTIN POGREBIN, B. 1939

Life shrinks or expands in proportion to one's courage.

ANAÏS NIN (1903-1977)

Believe that you hav

To be a champ, you have to believe in yourself when nobody else will.

SUGAR RAY ROBINSON (1921-1989)

Whatever you want in life, other people are going to want, too. Believe in yourself enough to accept the idea that you have an equal right to it.

DIANE SAWYER, B. 1945

orth. You have.

HANNAH KLEIN

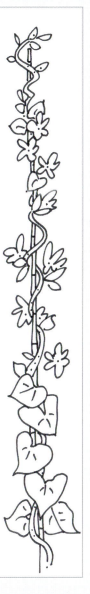

You have brains
in your head.
You have feet in
your shoes.
You can steer yourself
in any direction
you choose.
You're on your own.
And you know
what you know.
You are the guy who'll
decide where to go.

DR. SEUSS (1904-1991)

I wish you courage,

not only in the face of danger

– but in decisions.

Many a career never gets started,

for fear of failure.

HANNAH KLEIN,

Start where you are.

Use what you have.

Do what you can.

ARTHUR ASHE (1943-1993)

Life is a dream, realize it.
Life is a challenge, meet it.
Life is a duty, complete it.
Life is a game, play it.
Life is a promise, fulfil it.

MOTHER TERESA (1910-1997)

Start by doing what's necessary, then what's possible and suddenly you are doing the impossible.

ST. FRANCIS OF ASSISI (1181-1226)

Begin doing what you want to do now. We are not living in eternity. We have only this moment.

SIR FRANCIS BACON (1561-1626)

Trust yourself.
Create the kind of self
that you will be happy
to live with all your life.
Make the most of yourself
by fanning the tiny,
inner sparks of
possibility into flames
of achievement.

GOLDA MEIR (1898-1978)

Never be bullied into silence. Never allow yourself to be made a victim. Accept your definition of your life. Define yourself.

HARVEY FIERSTEIN, B. 1954

Believe in yourself
– even if no one else does!
Only you know, in your heart, what you can do.
Positive criticism, yes. Accept it gladly.
Denigration, no.

CHARLOTTE GRAY,

To be a success, you need more than just a competitive edge. You need a hide like a rhino, the ability to operate way outside normal comfort zones, a willingness to reinvent the rules, and total, utter, complete self-belief – against all odds. If you don't believe you can do it, why should anyone else?

LORD ALAN SUGAR, B. 1947

Mastering others is strength; mastering yourself is true power.

FROM "TAO TE CHING"

The people who get on in this world are the people who get up and look for the circumstances they want, and, if they can't find them, make them.

GEORGE BERNARD SHAW (1856-1950)

You've got to be energetic. You've got to have a passion which comes from every tentacle of your body, and you've got to make that passion a reality.

ANITA RODDICK (1942-2007)

Increase your happy times,
letting yourself go;
follow your desire
and best advantage.
And "do your thing"
while you are still
on this earth,
According to the command
of your heart.

AFRICAN PROVERB

Every day must come to you as a new hope, a new promise, a new aspiration. If you think that tomorrow will be just another day like all the days you have already seen, you will make no progress. Every day you have to energize yourself anew. For it is only with newness that you can succeed and transcend yourself.

SRI CHINMOY (1931-2007)

And you have to, down deep within the bottom of your soul, feel that you can do the job that you've set out to do.

WILLIAM DEVRIES, B. 1943

Some walks you have to take alone.

SUZANNE COLLINS

...you will discover your "alter ego".
That is the person inside of you
that is so committed
to achieving your goal
that you will become like
the strongest of laser beams,
capable of blowing away
any obstacle that stands in your way.

PETER EBDON, B. 1970

You've got to take
the initiative
and play your game.
In a decisive set,
confidence
is the difference.

CHRIS EVERT, B. 1954

If you believe in what you are doing,
then let nothing hold you up in your
work. Most of the great achievements
of the world have been done against
seeming impossibilities.

DALE CARNEGIE (1888-1955)

You can

do it. PAM BROWN (1928-2014)

*How many cares
one loses when one decides
not to be something,
but to be someone.*

COCO CHANEL (1883-1971)

*Shrug off the restraints
that you have allowed
others to place upon you.
You are limitless.
There is nothing you
cannot achieve.
There is no sadness in life
that cannot be reversed…*

CLEARWATER

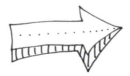

Nothing splendid has ever been achieved except by those who dared believe that something inside them was superior...

BRUCE BARTON

Give yourself a reason to believe in yourself.
Don't let what gifts you have
grow blunt and dull and useless.
Burnish them.
Explore and learn and practice.
Then you stand ready
 to snatch opportunities.
Then you can believe in your ability.

PAMELA DUGDALE

How can you hesitate?
Risk! Risk anything!
Care no more for
the opinion of others,
for those voices.
Do the hardest thing
on earth for you.
Act for yourself.
Face the truth.

KATHERINE MANSFIELD (1888-1923)

Some of us are timid.
We think we have something to lose
so we don't try for that next hill.

MAYA ANGELOU (1928-2014)

You are wiser
than you know,
cleverer than you know.
See what you can do
and be amazed.

HANNAH KLEIN

Above all, be the heroine of your life,
not the victim.

NORA EPHRON, B. 1941

Fortune favour

I was always looking outside myself for strength
and confidence but it comes from within.
It is there all the time.

ANNA FREUD (1895-1982)

…if you have the will, the luck, the time and the
energy, you can achieve everything.

TANNI GREY-THOMPSON, B. 1969

he brave.

TERENCE (c. 192 B.C.-157 B.C.)

*Our ordinary mind
always tries to persuade us
that we are nothing but acorns
and that our greatest happiness
will be to become bigger, fatter,
shinier acorns;
but that is of interest only
to pigs. Our faith gives
knowledge of something
much better; that we
can become oak trees.*

E. F. SCHUMACHER (1911-1977)

When you know yourself
you are empowered.
When you accept yourself
you are invincible.

TINA LIFFORD

I always did something
I was a little not ready to do.

MARISSA MAYER, B. 1975

*...once we believe
in ourselves,
we can risk curiosity,
wonder,
spontaneous delight,
or any experience
that reveals
the human spirit.*

E E CUMMINGS (1894-1962)

Saying yes means getting up
and acting on your belief
that you can create meaning
and purpose
in whatever life hands you.

SUSAN JEFFERS (1938-2012)

If you think you can, you can.
And if you think you can't, you're right.

MARY KAY ASH (1915-2001)

As you rush along the path towards your goals, stop from time to time to look back at where you have come from. Appreciate how far you have already travelled and what you have already achieved.

STUART & LINDA MACFARLANE

As long as you look for someone else to validate who you are by seeking their approval, you are setting yourself up for disaster. You have to be whole and complete in yourself. No one can give you that. You have to know who you are – what others say is irrelevant.

NIC SHEFF

Step into the unknown – live in it – and be prepared to hang out there. We cannot know what's in store for us, and by hanging on to what's familiar we block the new. Until hanging on by our fingertips to the old life, fed up with prising off our fingertips one by one, it simply kicks us into the abyss. As we fall screaming, it prepares a feather mattress for us. Stunned, we wonder why we didn't dive off to begin with. Live life. There's no waiting game. What is it you want to create right now? How do you want to be? Do it now.

CARON KEATING (1962-2004)

*Jump into the middle
of things,
get your hands dirty,
fall flat on your face,
and then reach
for the stars.*

JOAN L. CURCIO

Never let the future disturb you.
You will meet it, if you have to,
with the same weapons of reason which
today arm you against the present.

MARCUS AURELIUS (A.D. 121-180)

You have to risk
stepping outside
the circle
that has been drawn
around you.

LOURDES SAAB

While one person hesitates because of feeling inferior, the other is busy making mistakes and becoming superior.

HENRY C. LINK (1889-1952)

It is hard to fail, but it is worse never having tried to succeed.

THEODORE ROOSEVELT (1858-1919)

Success is the sum of small efforts...
Repeated day in and day out...
With never a thought of frustration...
With never a moment of doubt...

FLORENCE TAYLOR

Life is not easy for any of us.
But what of that?
We must have perseverance
and above all confidence
in ourselves.
We must believe
that we are gifted
for something,
and that this thing,
at whatever cost,
must be attained.

MARIE CURIE (1867-1934)

Risk more than others think is safe.
Care more than others think is wise.
Dream more than others think is practical.
Expect more than others think is possible.

CLAUDE BISSELL

*The moment
you doubt whether
you can fly,
you cease forever
to be able to do it.*

SIR JAMES M BARRIE (1860-1937)
FROM "PETER PAN"

The greatest mistake you can make in life is to be
continually fearing that you will make one.

ELBERT HUBBARD (1856-1915)

*Believe as though you are,
and you will be.*

ERNEST HOLMES (1887-1960)

*What I find
powerful is a person with
the confidence
to be her own self.*

OPRAH WINFREY, B. 1954

Believe in yourself,
take on your challenges,
dig deep within yourself to conquer fears.
Never let anyone bring you down.
You got to keep going.

CHANTAL SUTHERLAND, B. 1976

To feel valued, to know that you can do a job
well is an absolutely marvellous feeling.

BARBARA WALTERS, B. 1931

If life teaches us anything, it's maybe that it's necessary to suffer some defeats.

Look at a diamond: It is the result of extreme pressure. Less pressure, it is a crystal; less than that, it's coal; and less than that, it is fossilized leaves or just plain dirt. It's necessary, therefore, to be tough enough to bite the bullet as it is shot into one's mouth, to bite it and stop it before it tears a hole through one's throat.

One must learn to care for oneself first, so that one can then dare to care for someone else.

That's what it takes to make the caged bird sing.

MAYA ANGELOU (1928-2014)

Lighten up on yourself. No one is perfect. Gently accept your humanness.

DEBORAH DAY

The will to win, the desire to succeed, the urge to reach your full potential... these are the keys that will unlock the door to personal excellence.

CONFUCIUS (551 B.C. - 479 B.C.)

It is not the mountain we conquer but ourselves.

SIR EDMUND HILLARY (1919-2008)

Don't ever give up.
Believe in yourself
or no one else will.
My personal saying is:
I'd rather die knowing
that I tried to do
what I love.

ADRIENNE BAILON, B. 1983

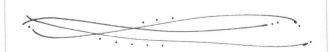

You can!

You can!

You did!!

STUART & LINDA MACFARLANE

Dance for yourself, if someone understands, good. If not then no matter, go right on doing what you love.

LOIS HURST

As is our confidence, so is our capacity.

WILLIAM HAZLITT (1778-1830)

To be beautiful means to be yourself.
You don't need to be accepted by others.
You need to accept yourself.

THICH NHAT HANH, B. 1926

If you hear a voice within you say "You are not a painter," then by all means paint, and that voice will be silenced.

VINCENT VAN GOGH (1853-1890)

*The turning point
in the process
of growing up is when
you discover
the core of strength
within you that
survives all hurt.*

MAX LERNER (1902-1992)

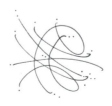

Most great men and women started small.
They knew rebuffs and disappointments
– but held on, believing in themselves.
Studied, thought and worked and hoped.
Until at last they found the recognition
they deserved.

CHARLOTTE GRAY

To be yourself in a world that is constantly
trying to make you something else
is the greatest achievement.

RALPH WALDO EMERSON (1803-1882)

It is time for every one of us to roll up our
sleeves and put ourselves at the top of our
commitment list.

MARIAN WRIGHT EDELMAN, B. 1939

*We cannot escape fear.
We only transform it into
a companion that
accompanies us on all our
exciting adventures…
Take a risk a day –
one small or bold stroke
that will make you feel great
once you have done it.*

SUSAN JEFFERS (1938-2012)

The beauty of life is that you never actually know what is going to happen to you when you wake up in the morning. So don't get stuck in routines. Don't get stuck, period. Embrace chance.

TAMARA CONNIFF

If you are insecure, guess what? The rest of the world is too. Do not overestimate the competition and underestimate yourself. You are better than you think.

T. HARV EKER, B. 1954

First say to yourself what you would be: and then do what you have to do.

EPICTETUS (c.55-135)

...victory is often a thing deferred, and rarely at the summit of courage... What is at the summit of courage, I think, is freedom.

The freedom that comes with the knowledge that no earthly power can break you; that an unbroken spirit is the only thing you cannot live without; that in the end it is the courage of conviction that moves things, that makes all change possible.

PROFESSOR PAULA GIDDINGS, B. 1947

Do not worry if you have built your castles in the air.
They are where they should be.
Now put the foundations under them.

HENRY DAVID THOREAU (1817-1862)

...human beings are often capable of greater things than they perform. They are sent into the world with bills of credit, and seldom draw them to their full extent.

HORACE WALPOLE (1717-1797)

*Some people say
I have attitude –
maybe I do.
But I think you have to.
You have to believe
in yourself
when no one else does –
that makes you a winner right there.*

VENUS WILLIAMS, B. 1980

As soon as you trust yourself,
you will know how to live.

JOHANN WOLFGANG VON GOETHE (1749-1832)

*Twenty years from now
you will be more
disappointed by the things
that you didn't do
than the ones you did do.
So throw off the bowlines.
Sail away from safe harbor.
Catch the trade winds
in your sails.*

*Explore.
Dream.
Discover.*

MARK TWAIN (1835-1910)

*T*he fact that courage
is expected of you
in the face of
the unbearable
gives you strength
for the rest of your life.

NELSON ROLIHLAHLA MANDELA (1918-2013)

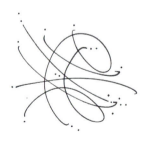